MW00989712

Trust Fall

Finding Confidence in God's Process

Brittany Rust

DEDICATION

Always striving to trust in Your process.

CONTENTS

Acknowledgments

ACKNOWLEDGMENTS

I know the challenges faced as a believer and that trusting God isn't always the natural or easy choice. However, learning to trust God is one of the most valuable lessons you can learn in this life.

You are created to flourish in this life and you can.

WELCOME TO THE JOURNEY

Two days after Ryan proposed to me on top of a mountain, I flew back home to Springfield, Missouri while he stayed in Colorado to start building a life for us in a new city. It was the longest two months of my life as I tied up loose ends where I was and planned the wedding of our dreams.

Don't get me wrong; planning a wedding was my jam and it was a blast! But going eight long weeks without seeing my fiancé was incredibly hard.

The reunion plan we had arranged included him flying into town on a Thursday night, taking our engagement pictures that Friday, and Saturday loading up the moving truck to head West. Our schedule held little room for things to go differently but being the type A planner that I am, I arranged all the details so that we'd have a smooth transition.

However, the weather didn't get my memo and things started to go awry.

That Thursday night bad weather hit from Colorado to Missouri and my fiancé's flight to Springfield was cancelled.

"*Breathe Britt. Don't panic!*" I gave myself a pep talk while I finished packing up the last few boxes in my apartment.

Ryan found out he could catch a flight to a town 3 hours from where I was so he called and asked if I was up for a road trip. Of course I was; anything to see his face once again! At 7 PM that Thursday night I hopped into my car and started driving west.

"*We can do this!*" I thought with excitement.

Ryan called again an hour into the drive and said the flight had been cancelled but that he could get a flight into our hometown the next day. It would put him in an hour before our photo shoot but it would work.

I pulled off the side of the highway into a little gravel lot in Oklahoma and I began to sob. It was a full on ugly cry.

"*God, why isn't this working out?*"
"*This is so important to me; don't you care?*"
"*Why are you doing this to me?!*"

I broke down in my car and became angry with Him for letting me down. For allowing everything to go wrong. I wanted to tell Him how disappointed I was.

On the side of that dark and lonely road, the Holy Spirit spoke to my confused heart and said,

"Trust in His process."

Over and over he spoke it to me until I began to recite it to myself. Until I began to believe it deep down. I had to trust God's process.

There will be times in your life when things don't go as planned. Or when you'll hit a life storm that beats you down in more ways than one. It's easy in those moments to get upset at God and question His plan. But it's also in those moments when your faith is tested.

How will you respond? Like me in anger or as the Holy Spirit would have you in faith?

This study will help you walk a journey to trusting God's process and plan. Giving you confidence that God is working all things for good and that He has a plan for your life.

Praying you have a refreshing journey and learn to trust all the edges of His ways!

Brittany

****

Before jumping into the study, take a moment and watch this short video I made just for you!

Link: www.brittanyrust.com/trust-fall-video
Password: trusttheprocess

SCARED TO TRUST

Psalm 9:10 (ESV)
"And those who know your name put their trust in you, for *you, O Lord, have not forsaken those who seek you.*"

When my now husband, Ryan, and I broke up in 2012, it was very clear we would never get back together. He moved on to dating another woman and I still fumbled through the healing process, finally moving on from my broken heart.

It was a move of God we started dating again 7 months later! But it wasn't easy. When we started talking again and having conversations about dating, I was scared. My heart had been so broken the first time it didn't work out and I was scared of going through it again. I wasn't sure I could take another let down of the heart. Trusting him again was a big step, hoping for the best.

Have you been hurt before? Perhaps someone close hurt you; someone you thought you could trust. Maybe it wasn't a person. Maybe you asked God to show up in a particularly difficult situation and He didn't work the way you wanted Him to. So now you're struggling with doubts about His ability to be there for you.

I know how much it hurts when trust is broken or someone didn't come through as you had hoped. Trying to trust anyone else again is a big ask for your broken heart.

People will let you down. Expectations won't be met. Situations will go awry. It's a surety in this life we can't escape.

However, there is someone you can trust--completely and wholeheartedly--with your life, hopes, and heart. His name is God but He also goes by Friend, Savior, Father, and Redeemer, just to name a few.

If you fall into the category where you asked God to show up and He didn't work as you had asked, that doesn't mean He isn't trustworthy. It just means He sees a greater good in the bigger picture only He can see. Always remember that God only does good. Even the bad that happens to you He can take and weave into a beautiful story.

I want you to take Psalm 9:10 as a promise to hold onto. A word of truth for you today. God will not forsake you. The good news is you can trust Him with everything--always.

If you're afraid to trust right now, it's time to have victory over that fear and learn to trust again. To trust God Almighty. He is a safe place for your heart and

He cares more deeply for you than you could ever imagine.

Will you take a leap of faith and trust again?

Reflection Questions

1. Why is it you are struggling to trust again? Use the space below to express why trust is hard for you.

2. Do you believe God can be trusted? If you're struggling at all to embrace this promise, right out Psalm 9:10 below. If you need some reminders throughout the week, right this verse down on a piece of paper and place in a spot you will see it often.

This One Thing
GOD WILL NOT FORSAKE YOU.

Journal Your Thoughts

_____

_____

_____

_____

_____

_____

WHY TRUSTING IS IMPORTANT

Proverbs 3:5-10 (ESV),

"Trust in the Lord with all your heart, and do not lean on your own understanding. In all your ways acknowledge him, and he will make straight your paths. Be not wise in your own eyes; fear the Lord, and turn away from evil. It will be healing to your flesh and refreshment to your bones. Honor the Lord with your wealth and with the firstfruits of all your produce; then your barns will be filled with plenty, and your vats will be bursting with wine."

Trust can be delicate and challenging to find. Most people have pieces of history when someone let them down or took advantage of them. There was existing trust extended to another and that trust was shattered in the aftermath of betrayal. It doesn't matter who you are; I've witnessed a scale where pastors limit their circle in extreme lengths after betrayal to people shutting those that love them most out to avoid loss again.

Trust is one of the most important attributes of the Christian walk. Trusting God and His process is key to our faith journey, and yet for most of us, our experiences in our past can leave us scared to death or unsure of how to trust. This study will walk you through a trust journey, however, you must first understand why it's important.

Proverbs 3:5-10 is an exploration of that why. The first step in our journey is to acknowledge our God and His plans. An understanding of the power, depth, and perfection of His plan must be acknowledged by you and me. When we can embrace that His plan and process is the best possible journey to be on, something happens. God MAKES our path straight.

There is a direct correlation between acknowledging Him and the direction of our lives. I know it can be hard to trust the invisible and unforeseen, but you must extend your trust to God. When you don't do that you are taking your future out of the hands of the Almighty and placing it into a dangerous place...the world.

Take some time to meditate on today's verses and come to terms with where your trust must lie. Do that and watch God go above and beyond your expectations.

I learned this the hard way three years ago (as you read about in my opening letter). I truly learned to embrace one statement: "I trust in Your process." I am continually reciting this phrase in my mind when I don't understand the situation I am facing. Because I don't understand or don't know what will happen, trust is necessary. It's not something I decided to do once and have not hesitated to do since; I must continually remind myself in the unknown that God has a plan, He is in control, and He has my best interests at heart. So, all I have is trust.

It's that important in your life--to trust.

Reflection Questions

1. Has there been a time in your life when you leaned on your own understanding and you saw how little you actually knew about the situation when it didn't quite work out as you had planned? What happened?

2. Have you witnessed a time in your life when you took a step of faith and God moved? Write out what that experience was and how you felt on the other side of that provision.

This One Thing
TRUST IN GOD'S PROCESS.

Journal Your Thoughts

_____

_____

_____

_____

_____

TRUST IS IMPORTANT TO GOD

Psalm 20:7 (ESV),

"Some trust in chariots and some in horses, but we trust in the name of the Lord our God."

It's not only important to understand why trust is important as a whole, but why specifically trust is important to God.

Psalm 20:7 identifies that many will trust in the world and the things it has to offer. Perhaps it's for this very reason trust is so important to God--because few do. Many want to put their confidence in financial security and jobs. But as we know, all things in this world are temporary. Only God is faithful beyond time.

Trust is an indicator of your heart's condition, reflecting where your loyalty and commitment lies. Trusting God in the midst of your trials and storms shows Him that you count on Him, not the world. That when offered the choice to make things work by the means this world offers or rely on God, you will choose to rely on God.

God wants full reliance on Him; He wants His children to lean in close and tap into the strength only He offers.

I can't help but wonder if some of the difficulties in our life are for this very reason; so that we learn to trust God. When I faced my own fork in the road last year, coming out of it I couldn't help but think I went through all of it just so I could learn to trust God to a greater degree. Even today a battle arose from the enemy to attack me as a writer; someone threatening to tarnish my character because they didn't like what I wrote. This morning I battled, wondering if I should give into their words.

Thankfully I had godly counsel around to encourage me to trust what God had called me to do. If God has called me to share my testimony through writing, I must hold firm to that conviction. Otherwise, I would be bending to the world instead of remaining steady to the course He has marked out before me.

Are you facing a battle that is calling out your trust? Perhaps someone is coming against you as well. Or maybe there is a situation at work that confronts you to operate out of fear. Whatever it is, may your heart reflect today your commitment to God in the middle of the conflict.

Choose today to be someone committed to the calling, purpose, and God-ordained direction on your life. Few will choose this path but to those who do, watch God paint your story with vibrant colors only reserved for those who are faithful, loyal, and fully committed to Him.

Reflection Questions

1. Are you finding yourself depending on something in this world? A job, bank account, or person. What is getting in the way of you fully trusting God and how will you overcome this obstacle?

2. How do you plan to show God that your trust is in Him? Will it be praying more consistently or finding promises in His word, just to name a few examples?

This One Thing
ONLY GOD IS FAITHFUL BEYOND TIME.

Journal Your Thoughts

_____

_____

_____

_____

_____

_____

THE DANGER OF
NOT TRUSTING GOD

Proverbs 11:28 (NLT),
"Trust in your money and down you go! But the godly flourish like leaves in spring."

Proverbs 28:26 (MSG),
"If you think you know it all, you're a fool for sure; real survivors learn wisdom from others."

You will have moments in life that test your faith and commitment to God. Because you are not perfect chances are you will give into the weakness a time or two. Your flesh will decide to take the path of least resistance and the world will be your guide. I'm so thankful that in those moments God's mercy and grace are abounding and generous!

However, please understand that there are consequences to your sin and disobedience.

The Bible mentions time and again stories of godly people who failed to trust God in moments of hardship. Abram claimed his wife as his sister more than once out of fear of men. Moses struck the rock in Numbers 20 in disobedience and, as a result, was not allowed to enter into the promised land. David sinned and tried to cover it up with more sin. We've all been there and we've all also experienced the results of not trusting God.

There are consequences when we decide to do things our way instead of God's.

Proverbs 11:28 speaks to the result of trusting in riches (and other things in this world) instead of God. The verse says that when we do this we will fall. No doubt that trusting in the world leads to failure. On the flip side, the godly flourish! Those who trust God will thrive regardless what comes their way.

Furthermore, Proverbs 28:26 says that those who are wise enough to trust in Him will be kept safe, as opposed to those who trust in themselves. Here the correlation is that when we decide to trust God there is a safety around us. How encouraging is that?! Such a blessing to know we have God on our side through thick and thin.

Today isn't meant to be a fear tactic, but a wise warning to the inevitable consequences of trusting in yourself or the world. I've found that to be true and you probably have too, but my prayer is that you don't have to face those consequences again. This is a reminder to keep your trust in God through the good, the bad, and the ugly. You will always regret not trusting Him, but you will never regret having done so.

Reflection Questions
1. Reflect back to a time you when you put your trust in yourself. How did that work out for you and what was it like?

2. Knowing things work out better if God is in control, does this make you want to lean into Him more? How so?

This One Thing
DON'T RELY ON YOURSELF--LEAN INTO THE FATHER.

Journal Your Thoughts

_____

_____

_____

_____

_____

_____

_____

WHY YOU SHOULD TRUST GOD

Psalm 9:10 (ESV),

"And those who know your name put their trust in you, for you, O Lord, have not forsaken those who seek you."

The benefits of trusting God are immeasurable. While the Bible is filled with stories of those who didn't trust God, it is also packed with stories of those who did! Daniel was thrown into the lion's den and came out alive, prompting the king to worship God. David faced Goliath and conquered the giant. Esther came before the king even though it could result in death and saved a nation. Shadrach, Meshach, and Abednego walked into the blazing furnace and came out without a single cinched hair.

Trusting in God has that kind of power. A kind of power that isn't just reserved for those in the Bible, but a power that's still active today for you and me. A power that bends the knees of kings to worship, conquers giants, saves nations, and protects individuals.

Psalm 9:10 testifies to this power. For those who put

their trust in God, He does not forsake them. This means that God will be with you in the trust journey and that's a promise you can always depend on. He will not give up, turn on you, or go back on His word. He will protect, defend, and honor you as long as you are His.

If there is one thing or person in this world you can count on, it's our Almighty God. The Creator of all things, Who sees the beginning and the end. Our God wants to show up for you and take care of your circumstances.

Maybe right now you're facing a situation that is calling for all the trust you can muster. The enemy may whisper sweet nothings into your ear to tempt you away from what is good and right, however, you must stand firm in truth.

Trust God's process. No matter how many times you must say this until you believe, say it.

The benefits of doing this will outshine what you can see this side of Heaven, but mostly, God will be on your side. Go with that knowledge as you make your decision to follow God and trust Him.

Reflection Questions

1. Can you remember a time when God did show up for you? What was that experience like?

2. Do you trust Him to do the same again?

This One Thing
GOD WILL NOT FORSAKE YOU.

Journal Your Thoughts

_____

_____

_____

_____

_____

_____

_____

_____

_____

_____

DEVELOPING TRUST

Psalm 13:5 (NLT),

"But I trust in your unfailing love. I will rejoice because you have rescued me."

Solid trust starts with relationship. It begins with a commitment to know each other and be there for each other. The beautiful thing about God is that He is always extending the opportunity to be in relationship with Him and as we know, He is completely trustworthy.

Psalm 13:5 tells us of His unfailing love. A love that never ends and never gives up on us, no matter what we've done. When you put your trust in that--into something that never ends--your trust is safe and in the right place.

This verse also reminds us that He rescues. He's there for us. Defends us. All these things we're talking about--His rescuing love--is found in relationship with Him. The closer you draw to Him, the closer He will draw to you. And with that intimacy you will find that there is no one like Him. You'll believe what He says in His word. In that relationship, trust is formed.

If you don't yet have a relationship with Jesus, ask him to be the Lord of your life. Make a commitment today to follow him as long as you live. Make him your number one!

If you do have a relationship, it's time to take it to the next level. If you're reading this study, chances are you're looking to trust Him to a greater degree. If that's what you desire, it means drawing closer and going deeper.

There's no formula to relationship but I can give you a few things you can do to grow in intimacy with Him.

1. *Make prayer and worship consistent.*
2. *Be in His word daily.*
3. *Engage in community with other believers.*
4. *Operate out of the Holy Spirit.*

If you can make these spiritual disciplines a priority in your life, you will find yourself in a deeper relationship with God that fosters unwavering trust. The closer you get to Him, the less likely you are to waver in trust when the going gets tough.

Be in relationship with God and find trust in His unfailing love.

Reflection Questions

1. On a scale of 1 to 10, one being far away and ten being incredibly close, how would you rate your relationship to God right now.

2. How can you grow closer to Him? Is there one thing from the list above that you would like to be more strategic about?

This One Thing
PURSUE INTIMACY WITH GOD.

Journal Your Thoughts

_____

_____

_____

_____

_____

_____

_____

WHEN TRUST IS TESTED

Psalm 56:3 (ESV),
"When I am afraid, I put my trust in you. "

Romans 15:13 (NLT),
"I pray that God, the source of hope, will fill you completely with joy and peace because you trust in him. Then you will overflow with confident hope through the power of the Holy Spirit."

What if trusting God in the unforeseen challenges is more difficult than it sounds? This is likely to be true at times. And when that happens you will have to gather everything inside of you to muster up trust. It may not be easy, but it will be necessary for staying on track.

In Psalm 56:3 God says that when you are afraid you must put your trust in Him. There is no other option in who to trust and there is no other way through the fear. Plain and simple, it's trust you have to gather when the flesh fights to tap out when the going gets too tough.

In addition, Romans 15:13 states that you will be filled with peace BECAUSE you trusted in God. No claims that the peace comes before trusting, only after trusting. Which means when you're searching for peace in the midst of your struggle the only way to find it is if you put your trust in God!

How do you keep trusting when you're afraid?

Just do it!

I know it sounds too easy, but it can be done. As I said on week one, I constantly tell myself over and over in times of struggle to, "trust in God's process." I'll say it until all I can do is believe it. I'll also speak verses that apply to the situation over myself because there is no weapon stronger to fight the enemy with than the Word of God and in the name of Jesus.

My prayer is that as you read this you'll find that trust in God and His process. When it gets tough, and it will, come back to speaking Scripture over yourself. Turn to God in your fear. Call out to Him when the trust is fading. When you do that, when you seek to put your trust in Him, He will give you peace. He will honor that and not forsake you. There is nothing stronger than the words and promises of our Almighty God.

Reflection Questions
1. What are you afraid of right now? Health, money, relationships? Write out what that is and then put a big "X" through the writing and declare that you are going to put your trust in Him.

2. What does peace in the middle of your storm look like? Do you believe God is able to provide that to you?

This One Thing
THERE IS PEACE WHEN YOU TRUST GOD.

Journal Your Thoughts

_____

_____

_____

_____

_____

_____

YOU ARE NOT ALONE

Hebrews 11 (NLT),

"Faith shows the reality of what we hope for; it is the evidence of things we cannot see. Through their faith, the people in days of old earned a good reputation. By faith we understand that the entire universe was formed at God's command, that what we now see did not come from anything that can be seen.

It was by faith that Abel brought a more acceptable offering to God than Cain did. Abel's offering gave evidence that he was a righteous man, and God showed his approval of his gifts. Although Abel is long dead, he still speaks to us by his example of faith.

It was by faith that Enoch was taken up to heaven without dying—'he disappeared, because God took him.' For before he was taken up, he was known as a person who pleased God. And it is impossible to please God without faith. Anyone who wants to come to him must believe that God exists and that he rewards those who sincerely seek him.

It was by faith that Noah built a large boat to save his family from the flood. He obeyed God, who warned him about things that had never happened before. By his faith Noah condemned the rest of the world, and he received the righteousness that comes by faith.

It was by faith that Abraham obeyed when God called him to leave home and go to another land that God would give him as his inheritance. He went without knowing where he was going. And even when he reached the land God promised him, he lived there by faith—for he was like a foreigner, living in tents. And so did Isaac and Jacob, who inherited the same promise. Abraham was confidently looking forward to a city with eternal foundations, a city designed and built by God.

It was by faith that even Sarah was able to have a child, though she was barren and was too old. She believed that God would keep his promise. And so a whole nation came from this one man who was as good as dead—a nation with so many people that, like the stars in the sky and the sand on the seashore, there is no way to count them.

All these people died still believing what God had promised them. They did not receive what was promised, but they saw it all from a distance and welcomed it. They agreed that they were foreigners and nomads here on earth. Obviously people who say such things are looking forward to a country they can call their own. If they had longed for the country they came from, they could have gone back. But they were looking for a better place, a heavenly homeland. That is why God is not ashamed to be called their God, for he has prepared a city for them.

It was by faith that Abraham offered Isaac as a sacrifice when God was testing him. Abraham, who had received God's promises, was ready to sacrifice his only son, Isaac, even though God had told him, "Isaac is the son through whom your descendants will be counted." Abraham reasoned that if Isaac died, God was able to bring him back to life again. And in a

29

sense, Abraham did receive his son back from the dead.

It was by faith that Isaac promised blessings for the future to his sons, Jacob and Esau.

It was by faith that Jacob, when he was old and dying, blessed each of Joseph's sons and bowed in worship as he leaned on his staff.

It was by faith that Joseph, when he was about to die, said confidently that the people of Israel would leave Egypt. He even commanded them to take his bones with them when they left.

It was by faith that Moses' parents hid him for three months when he was born. They saw that God had given them an unusual child, and they were not afraid to disobey the king's command.

It was by faith that Moses, when he grew up, refused to be called the son of Pharaoh's daughter. He chose to share the oppression of God's people instead of enjoying the fleeting pleasures of sin. He thought it was better to suffer for the sake of Christ than to own the treasures of Egypt, for he was looking ahead to his great reward. It was by faith that Moses left the land of Egypt, not fearing the king's anger. He kept right on going because he kept his eyes on the one who is invisible. It was by faith that Moses commanded the people of Israel to keep the Passover and to sprinkle blood on the doorposts so that the angel of death would not kill their firstborn sons.

It was by faith that the people of Israel went right through the Red Sea as though they were on dry ground. But when the Egyptians tried to follow, they were all drowned. It was by faith that the people of Israel marched around Jericho for seven days, and the walls came crashing down.

*It was by faith that Rahab the prostitute was not destroyed
with the people in her city who refused to obey God. For she
had given a friendly welcome to the spies.*

*How much more do I need to say? It would take too long to
recount the stories of the faith of Gideon, Barak, Samson,
Jephthah, David, Samuel, and all the prophets. By faith these
people overthrew kingdoms, ruled with justice, and received what
God had promised them. They shut the mouths of lions,
quenched the flames of fire, and escaped death by the edge of the
sword. Their weakness was turned to strength. They became
strong in battle and put whole armies to flight. Women received
their loved ones back again from death.*

*But others were tortured, refusing to turn from God in order to
be set free. They placed their hope in a better life after the
resurrection. Some were jeered at, and their backs were cut open
with whips. Others were chained in prisons. Some died by
stoning, some were sawed in half, and others were killed with
the sword. Some went about wearing skins of sheep and goats,
destitute and oppressed and mistreated. They were too good for
this world, wandering over deserts and mountains, hiding in
caves and holes in the ground.*

*All these people earned a good reputation because of their faith,
yet none of them received all that God had promised. For God
had something better in mind for us, so that they would not
reach perfection without us."*

Reflection Questions
1. Which character stood out to you most and why?

2. Do you believe that if God did it for them, He will do it for you?!

This One Thing
YOU ARE NOT ALONE.

Journal Your Thoughts

_____

_____

_____

_____

_____

_____

_____

_____

_____

ABOUT THE AUTHOR

Brittany Rust is a writer, speaker and pastor at Red Rocks Church in Colorado. The author of Untouchable: Unraveling the Myth That You're Too Faithful to Fall and a contributor for Propel Women, Crosswalk, iBelieve, YouVersion, and Single Christianity magazine, she also hosts the Epic Fails podcast. Her passion is to give encouragement to the world-weary believer through her writing, speaking and podcasting. Brittany and her husband Ryan live with their handsome son Roman and a lab in Castle Rock, Colorado. Learn more at www.brittanyrust.com.

Made in the USA
Middletown, DE
22 July 2019